Embrace Your Wealth:

Mastering Financial Success and Eliminating Money Worries

Daniel C. Partin

Table of content

Introduction

Chapter 1: Understanding the Power of Money Mindset

What is a money mindset?

How your money mindset affects your financial success

The importance of embracing wealth

Chapter 2: Building a Solid Financial Foundation

Setting financial goals

Budgeting basics

Creating an emergency fund

Understanding debt and managing it wisely

Chapter 3: Investing for Long-Term Financial Success

The basics of investing

Different types of investments

Creating an investment strategy

Managing risk in your portfolio

Chapter 4: Mastering Your Relationship with Money

Identifying your financial values

Overcoming limiting beliefs about money
Changing negative money habits
Practicing gratitude and abundance
Chapter 5: Increasing Your Income and
Creating Multiple Streams of Income
Advancing in your career
Starting a side business or freelancing
Investing in real estate or other passive
income streams
Building a personal brand and monetizing
your skills
Chapter 6: Protecting Your Wealth and
Planning for the Future
Estate planning basics
Protecting your assets with insurance
Retirement planning and saving for the
future
Legacy planning and charitable giving
Conclusion

Introduction

In today's world, financial success and security have become paramount to living a comfortable and stress-free life. However, the path to achieving financial stability is often riddled with obstacles and challenges that can leave even the most financially savvy individuals feeling overwhelmed and uncertain. This is where "Embrace Your Wealth: Mastering Financial Success and Eliminating Money Worries" comes in.

This book is a comprehensive guide that aims to help readers understand and navigate the complex world of personal finance. Whether you are just starting on your financial journey or looking to improve your current financial situation, "Embrace Your Wealth" provides practical and actionable advice that will help you achieve your goals.

Through this book, you will learn how to create a financial plan that is tailored to your individual needs, identify and overcome common financial mistakes and pitfalls, and develop healthy habits that will enable you to build and maintain long-term financial success. The book also covers topics such as budgeting, investing, and debt management, providing readers with the knowledge and tools they need to make informed financial decisions.

"Embrace Your Wealth" is more than just a book about managing money; it is a mindset shift that will help you view money in a positive and empowering light. By embracing your wealth and mastering financial success, you can eliminate money worries and live a life of abundance and financial security.

Chapter 1: Understanding the Power of Money Mindset

What is a money mindset?

A money mindset refers to an individual's beliefs, attitudes, and perceptions about money and wealth. It includes their thoughts and feelings about their ability to make money, manage it effectively, and achieve financial goals. A positive money mindset is characterized by beliefs and attitudes that support financial success, such as confidence in one's ability to create wealth, a willingness to take calculated risks, and a focus on abundance rather than scarcity. Conversely, a negative money mindset is characterized by limiting beliefs and attitudes that hinder financial success, such as fear, scarcity mentality, and self-doubt. Developing a positive money mindset can be beneficial for achieving financial success and creating a fulfilling life.

How your money mindset affects your financial success

Your money mindset, or your beliefs and attitudes about money, can have a significant impact on your financial success. Your mindset can influence your financial decisions, your ability to earn and save money, and your overall financial well-being.

Here are some ways that your money mindset can affect your financial success:

Limiting beliefs can hold you back: If you have negative beliefs about money, such as believing that money is evil or that it's impossible to get ahead financially, these beliefs can limit your ability to take action and achieve financial success. It's important to recognize and challenge these limiting beliefs in order to move past them and take positive steps towards financial success.

A scarcity mindset can lead to poor financial decisions: If you believe that there's never enough money to go around, you may be more likely to make poor financial decisions, such as overspending or taking on too much debt. A scarcity mindset can also make it difficult to save money and invest in your future.

A growth mindset can lead to financial success: On the other hand, if you have a growth mindset and believe that you can learn and grow your financial knowledge and skills, you're more likely to take positive steps towards financial success. This might include investing in your education, seeking out financial advice, and taking calculated risks to grow your wealth.

Money can impact your self-worth:
For some people, their self-worth is tied to their net worth. If you believe that your value as a person is tied to your financial success, you may be more likely to take on too much debt, overspend, or engage in other risky financial behaviors in order to maintain your self-worth.

Your mindset can impact your earning potential: Your beliefs about money can also impact your earning potential. For example, if you believe that you're not worthy of a higher salary or that it's not possible to earn more money, you may be less likely to negotiate for a higher salary or take on opportunities to increase your income.

Overall, your money mindset can have a significant impact on your financial success. By recognizing and challenging limiting beliefs, adopting a growth mindset, and prioritizing your financial well-being, you can take positive steps towards achieving your financial goals.

The importance of embracing wealth

The concept of wealth is often associated with the accumulation of money, assets, and material possessions. While there are certainly negative connotations that come with the pursuit of wealth, it's important to recognize that there are also many benefits to embracing wealth in a responsible and balanced way. In this response, we'll explore some of the reasons why wealth can be an important component of a fulfilling life.

Financial security: One of the most obvious benefits of wealth is the ability to provide financial security for oneself and one's loved ones. This includes having a comfortable home, reliable transportation, access to quality healthcare, and the ability to cover unexpected expenses. Financial security allows individuals to focus on other aspects of their lives without constantly worrying about how they'll make ends meet.

Increased opportunities: Wealth can also open up a wider range of opportunities, both personally and professionally. For example, having the financial resources to pursue higher education or start a business can lead to greater success and fulfillment in one's career. It can also provide the resources to travel, experience new cultures, and broaden one's horizons.

Improved quality of life: With wealth often comes an improved quality of life. This can include access to better healthcare, healthier food options, and opportunities for leisure activities. Wealth can also provide the resources to pursue hobbies and interests, leading to a more fulfilling and enjoyable life overall.

Giving back: Wealth can also provide individuals with the resources to give back to their communities and make a positive impact on the world. Philanthropy and charitable giving are important ways that individuals with wealth can make a difference in the lives of others and contribute to society.

Legacy building: For many individuals, building and preserving wealth is a way to leave a legacy for future generations. This can include passing down assets to family members, establishing charitable foundations, or contributing to causes that align with one's values and beliefs.

It's important to note that the pursuit of wealth should be balanced with other aspects of life, such as personal relationships, physical and mental health, and spiritual fulfillment. Pursuing wealth at the expense of these other areas can lead to a shallow and unfulfilling life. However, when pursued in a responsible and balanced way, wealth can provide individuals with the resources and opportunities to lead a fulfilling and impactful life.

Chapter 2: Building a Solid Financial Foundation

Setting financial goals

Setting financial goals is an important part of personal financial planning. Financial goals help you identify what you want to achieve financially and provide a roadmap for achieving those goals.

Importance of Setting Financial Goals:

Setting financial goals is essential for several reasons, including:

Provides direction and focus: Financial goals help provide direction and focus for your financial planning. They help you prioritize your spending, saving, and investing activities to achieve your goals.

Measures progress: Setting financial goals allows you to track your progress towards achieving your financial objectives. It helps you evaluate your financial situation regularly and adjust your strategies if needed.

Motivates you to save and invest: Having specific financial goals can be motivating and encouraging. It gives you something to work towards and helps you stay focused on your long-term financial goals.

Reduces financial stress: Setting financial goals can help reduce financial stress. It gives you a sense of control over your finances and provides a framework for making financial decisions.

Types of Financial Goals:

There are several types of financial goals that you can set, including:

Short-term goals: These are financial goals that you want to achieve within the next 12 months, such as paying off credit card debt, saving for a vacation, or buying a new computer.

Medium-term goals: These are financial goals that you want to achieve within the next 1-5 years, such as saving for a down payment on a house, buying a new car, or starting a business.

Long-term goals: These are financial goals that you want to achieve in more than 5 years, such as saving for retirement, paying off a mortgage, or funding your children's education.

Tips for Setting Effective Financial Goals:

Here are some tips for setting effective financial goals:

Be specific: When setting financial goals, be as specific as possible. Instead of saying "save money," say "save $10,000 for a down payment on a house."

Be realistic: Make sure your financial goals are achievable. Setting unrealistic goals can be discouraging and lead to frustration.

Be time-bound: Set a deadline for achieving your financial goals. This will help you stay motivated and focused.

Break down larger goals into smaller ones: If you have a long-term financial goal, break it down into smaller, more manageable goals. This will make it easier to track your progress and stay motivated.

Make your goals visible: Write down your financial goals and keep them visible. This will serve as a reminder of what you're working towards.

Review and adjust regularly: Review your financial goals regularly and adjust them if needed. Life circumstances and financial situations can change, so it's important to stay flexible.

Budgeting basics

Budgeting is the process of creating a financial plan for an individual or organization that outlines expected income and expenses over a specific period. This plan helps to ensure that expenses don't exceed income, and resources are used in a responsible and effective way. We will discuss the basics of budgeting.

Determine your Income:
The first step in budgeting is to determine how much money you have coming in each month. This includes your salary or wages, any side hustles or part-time work, rental income, and any other sources of regular income.

List your Expenses:
The next step is to list all of your regular expenses. This includes fixed expenses like rent, utilities, insurance premiums, car payments, and other bills that you pay every

month. It also includes variable expenses such as groceries, entertainment, dining out, and other discretionary spending.

Categorize your Expenses:
After listing your expenses, you need to categorize them into different groups. This will help you see where your money is going and identify areas where you can cut back if needed. For example, you might have categories like housing, transportation, food, entertainment, and savings.

Set Financial Goals:
Once you have a clear understanding of your income and expenses, it's time to set financial goals. These can include short-term goals like saving for a vacation or long-term goals like saving for retirement. Set goals that are specific, measurable, achievable, relevant, and time-bound.

Allocate Funds:
After setting your financial goals, allocate funds to each category in your budget. You should prioritize your expenses based on your needs and financial goals. For example, allocate more funds to necessary expenses like rent and groceries and less to discretionary spending like entertainment.

Monitor your Budget:
Monitoring your budget is crucial to ensure that you are staying on track and achieving your financial goals. This can be done by reviewing your bank statements regularly, tracking your expenses, and adjusting your budget as needed.

Use Technology to help:
There are several budgeting tools and apps available that can help you track your expenses, set financial goals, and monitor your budget. These tools can automate the process and make it easier for you to manage your finances.

Creating an emergency fund

An emergency fund is a sum of money set aside specifically to deal with unexpected expenses or situations that may arise in the future. These could include things like medical bills, car repairs, job loss, or any other unforeseen circumstances that could impact your financial stability.

Creating an emergency fund is an important part of financial planning. Without one, unexpected expenses can quickly lead to financial stress and even debt. Here are some tips for creating an emergency fund:

Set a savings goal: The first step in creating an emergency fund is to set a savings goal. This will give you a target to aim for and help you stay motivated. A good rule of thumb is to save at least three to six months' worth of living expenses. This means if your monthly expenses are $3,000, your emergency fund should be between $9,000 to $18,000.

Make a budget: Creating a budget can help you identify areas where you can cut back on expenses and free up more money to put towards your emergency fund. Start by tracking your spending for a month or two to get a clear idea of where your money is going. Then, look for areas where you can reduce expenses, such as eating out less or canceling subscriptions you don't use.

Automate your savings: One of the easiest ways to save money is to automate it. Set up a recurring transfer from your checking account to your emergency fund savings account each month. This way, you don't have to remember to transfer the money yourself, and it becomes a habit.

Keep your emergency fund separate: It's important to keep your emergency fund separate from your other accounts, such as checking or savings accounts. This will help you avoid dipping into the funds for non-emergency purposes. Consider opening a high-yield savings account specifically for your emergency fund. This will help your money grow over time, and you can access it quickly if needed.

Revisit and adjust your savings plan: Once you've established your emergency fund, it's important to revisit your savings plan periodically to make sure you're on track to meet your goals. If you experience a significant life change, such as a job loss or a medical emergency, you may need to adjust your savings plan to account for these new circumstances.

Understanding debt and managing it wisely

Debt is an amount of money borrowed by an individual or organization from another individual, organization, or lender. It is a common way to finance various expenses, such as buying a home, a car, or starting a business. However, managing debt wisely is essential to avoid financial difficulties and maintain a healthy financial situation.

Understanding Debt:

Debt comes in various forms, including credit cards, personal loans, mortgages, and student loans. Each type of debt has different terms and conditions, including interest rates, payment schedules, and fees. It is important to understand the details of each loan or credit agreement before accepting it. This will help you to determine how much money you need to repay and when the payments are due.

Managing Debt Wisely:

Managing debt wisely means having a plan to pay off your debt and not taking on more debt than you can handle. Here are some tips for managing debt wisely:

Create a Budget: A budget is a plan that outlines your income and expenses. It can help you to track your spending and identify areas where you can cut back. Creating a budget is an essential step in managing debt wisely.

Prioritize High-Interest Debt:
High-interest debt, such as credit card debt, should be a priority when paying off debt. Paying off high-interest debt first can help you to save money on interest charges and reduce the overall amount of debt.

Make Payments on Time: Late payments can result in additional fees and penalties, which can increase your debt. Making payments on time is essential to maintaining a good credit score and avoiding unnecessary charges.

Consider Debt Consolidation: Debt consolidation involves combining multiple debts into one loan with a lower interest rate. This can make it easier to manage your debt and reduce your monthly payments.

Seek Professional Help: If you are struggling to manage your debt, consider seeking help from a financial advisor or credit counselor. They can provide advice on how to manage your debt and create a plan to pay it off.

Chapter 3: Investing for Long-Term Financial Success

The basics of investing

Investing is the process of committing money or capital with the expectation of receiving a financial return or profit in the future. Investing is important for individuals and businesses alike because it helps them grow their wealth over time. However, investing can be risky and complicated, especially for beginners. We will discuss the basics of investing to help you understand the key concepts and principles involved.

Set your investment goals: The first step in investing is to define your investment goals. What are you investing for? Is it for retirement, a down payment on a house, or to save for your children's college education? Once you have a clear understanding of your investment goals, you can determine the investment strategy that is best suited to achieve them.

Determine your risk tolerance: Every investment carries some degree of risk, and different investors have different levels of risk tolerance. It's important to determine your risk tolerance before investing so that you can select an investment strategy that aligns with your risk profile. Generally, the younger you are, the more risk you can take because you have more time to recover from losses.

Diversify your portfolio: Diversification is a risk management strategy that involves investing in different asset classes, industries, and geographical regions. By diversifying your portfolio, you can reduce the risk of loss from any single investment. Diversification can also increase your chances of earning a positive return on your investment.

Understand the different types of investments: There are several types of investments available, each with its own set of risks and potential rewards. The most common types of investments include stocks, bonds, mutual funds, exchange-traded funds (ETFs), real estate, and commodities. It's important to understand the risks and benefits of each investment type before investing.

Conduct research: Before investing, it's important to conduct research on the investment opportunities available to you. This can include analyzing the company's financial statements, researching industry trends, and reading analyst reports. The more you know about the investment, the better equipped you will be to make informed decisions.

Monitor your investments: Investing is not a set-it-and-forget-it activity. You need to monitor your investments regularly to ensure that they are performing as expected. You should also review your investment strategy periodically to make sure that it still aligns with your investment goals and risk tolerance.

Consider working with a financial advisor: Investing can be complex, and it's not uncommon for investors to make mistakes. Working with a financial advisor can help you make informed investment decisions and avoid costly mistakes. A financial advisor can also help you create an investment plan that aligns with your goals and risk profile.

Different types of investments

There are various types of investments, each with its unique characteristics and risks. Here are some of the different types of investments:

Stocks: Stocks represent ownership in a company, and when you buy a share of stock, you become a shareholder in that company. The value of a stock can increase or decrease based on various factors, including the company's financial performance, industry trends, and market conditions. Investing in stocks can provide the potential for high returns, but it also comes with a higher risk.

Bonds: Bonds are debt securities issued by corporations, municipalities, and governments. When you buy a bond, you're essentially loaning money to the issuer, who agrees to pay you back with interest over a specific period. Bonds offer lower returns than stocks, but they are generally considered less risky.

Real Estate: Real estate investing involves buying properties with the goal of generating rental income or capital appreciation. Real estate investments can include residential, commercial, and industrial properties, as well as real estate investment trusts (REITs), which are securities that invest in real estate.

Mutual Funds: A mutual fund is a professionally managed investment portfolio that pools money from many investors to purchase a diversified mix of stocks, bonds, or other assets. Mutual funds offer diversification and professional management, but they also come with fees and expenses.

Exchange-Traded Funds (ETFs): ETFs are similar to mutual funds but are traded on an exchange like a stock. They offer investors a low-cost, tax-efficient way to gain exposure to a diversified portfolio of stocks, bonds, or other assets.

Certificates of Deposit (CDs): CDs are fixed-income investments that offer a guaranteed rate of return for a specific period. CDs are considered low-risk investments, but they also offer lower returns than stocks and other higher-risk investments.

Commodities: Commodities are raw materials or primary agricultural products that can be bought and sold, such as gold, oil, and wheat. Investing in commodities can provide diversification and protection against inflation, but it also comes with risks such as volatility and limited upside potential.

Cryptocurrencies: Cryptocurrencies are digital assets that use encryption techniques to secure and verify transactions. They are highly volatile and speculative investments, with the potential for significant gains or losses.

Alternative Investments: Alternative investments are non-traditional investments that do not fit into any of the above categories. Examples include private equity, hedge funds, and art or collectibles. Alternative investments can offer higher returns but come with higher fees and greater risk.

Creating an investment strategy

Creating an investment strategy is a critical process for anyone looking to build long-term wealth. A good investment strategy will help you to identify your goals, risk tolerance, and time horizon, as well as the best assets to invest in to achieve those goals. Here are some key steps to consider when creating an investment strategy:

Determine your investment goals: The first step in creating an investment strategy is to determine your investment goals. Are you looking to generate passive income, save for retirement, or build long-term wealth? It's essential to identify your goals so that you can create a plan that aligns with them.

Assess your risk tolerance: Every investor has a different level of risk tolerance. Some investors are willing to take on more risk for the potential of higher returns, while others prefer a more conservative approach. It's important to assess your risk tolerance to determine the level of risk you're comfortable taking on.

Evaluate your time horizon: Your time horizon is the length of time you plan to hold your investments. If you have a long time horizon, you may be able to take on more risk, as you have more time to recover from any short-term losses. Conversely, if you have a short time horizon, you may want to consider a more conservative approach.

Determine your asset allocation: Asset allocation refers to the distribution of your investments across different asset classes, such as stocks, bonds, and real estate. The right asset allocation will depend on your investment goals, risk tolerance, and time horizon. For example, if you're looking to generate passive income, you may want to consider investing in real estate or dividend-paying stocks.

Choose your investments: Once you've determined your asset allocation, you'll need to choose the specific investments you want to make. This may involve researching individual stocks, mutual funds, or exchange-traded funds (ETFs). It's important to do your research and select investments that align with your investment goals and risk tolerance.

Monitor and adjust your portfolio: Once you've created your investment strategy and chosen your investments, it's essential to monitor your portfolio regularly and make adjustments as necessary. This may involve rebalancing your asset allocation, selling underperforming investments, or buying new ones.

Managing risk in your portfolio

Managing risk in your portfolio is an important aspect of investing. It involves strategies that help to minimize the potential for loss and to maximize returns. By taking a proactive approach to risk management, investors can achieve their investment objectives while minimizing potential losses. We will discuss some key strategies for managing risk in your portfolio.

Diversification: Diversification is a strategy that involves investing in a variety of assets in different industries and geographic regions. By spreading your investments across multiple asset classes, you reduce the risk of losing all of your investment in one particular security or industry. For example, if you invest only in the technology sector and there is a downturn in that sector, your entire portfolio could suffer. However, if you diversify your investments across multiple sectors such as technology, healthcare, consumer goods, etc. you may reduce the impact of any downturn in a particular industry.

Asset Allocation: Asset allocation is the process of dividing your investment portfolio among different asset classes such as stocks, bonds, and cash. This helps to balance risk and return. A well-balanced portfolio that is diversified across multiple asset classes can help to minimize the risk of loss in any one particular area. For example, if you have a high risk tolerance, you may allocate a larger portion of your portfolio to stocks. However, if you have a low risk tolerance, you may allocate a larger portion to bonds and cash.

Risk Appetite: Risk appetite is the level of risk that an investor is willing to take. It is important to consider your risk appetite when managing your portfolio. If you are risk-averse, you may prefer investments that offer lower returns but are more stable and predictable. On the other hand, if you have a higher risk appetite, you may be willing to take on more risk in pursuit of higher returns.

Rebalancing: Rebalancing is the process of adjusting your portfolio to maintain your desired asset allocation. Over time, the performance of different assets will vary, causing your portfolio to become unbalanced. Rebalancing involves selling investments that have performed well and buying investments that have underperformed in order to maintain your desired asset allocation. This helps to reduce the risk of being overexposed to any one particular asset class.

Hedging: Hedging is a strategy that involves taking a position that offsets the risk of an existing investment. This can be done through options, futures, or other financial instruments. For example, if you own a large number of shares in a particular stock, you may buy put options on that stock to protect yourself against a potential decline in the stock price.

Monitoring: Finally, it is important to regularly monitor your portfolio to ensure that it continues to align with your investment objectives and risk appetite. This involves reviewing your investments and assessing their performance relative to the market and your expectations. You should also consider changes in your personal circumstances such as changes in your income, expenses, or risk tolerance.

Chapter 4: Mastering Your Relationship with Money

Identifying your financial values

Identifying your financial values is an essential step in achieving financial stability and success. Your financial values are the guiding principles that shape your attitudes and behaviors towards money. They help you prioritize your financial goals and make better decisions about how to manage your finances.

Here are some tips on how to identify your financial values:

Reflect on your upbringing and experiences: Your upbringing and past experiences can have a significant impact on your financial values. Think about how your parents or guardians handled money, and what you learned from them. Reflect on your past experiences with money, both positive and negative, and how they have influenced your current financial beliefs and behaviors.

Determine your priorities: Think about what is most important to you in life. Is it security, freedom, or experiences? Knowing your priorities can help you set financial goals that align with them.

Evaluate your spending habits: Review your spending habits over the past few months or even a year. What types of expenses do you prioritize, and what do you tend to overspend on? This will give you insight into what you value most in terms of spending.

Consider your long-term goals: What are your long-term financial goals? Do you want to save for retirement, buy a home, or start a business? Understanding your long-term goals can help you make better financial decisions in the present.

Assess your risk tolerance: Your risk tolerance is your willingness to take on financial risks in pursuit of higher returns. Some people are more risk-averse, while others are comfortable taking on higher levels of risk. Knowing your risk tolerance can help you make investment decisions that align with your values and goals.

Once you have identified your financial values, you can use them as a guide for making financial decisions. For example, if you value security, you may prioritize building an emergency fund over investing in risky assets. If you value experiences, you may allocate more of your budget towards travel or entertainment.

Remember that your financial values may change over time as your priorities and goals evolve. It's important to regularly reassess your financial values to ensure that you're still on track to achieve your goals. By identifying your financial values, you can make more informed financial decisions and achieve greater financial stability and success.

Overcoming limiting beliefs about money

Limiting beliefs are beliefs that restrict us from achieving our full potential. When it comes to money, limiting beliefs can prevent us from earning more, saving, investing, and even enjoying money. These beliefs can be deeply ingrained in our minds, often developed from past experiences, upbringing, and societal expectations. However, it's important to recognize and overcome these beliefs to reach financial freedom and abundance.

Here are some ways to overcome limiting beliefs about money:

Identify your limiting beliefs: The first step to overcoming limiting beliefs is to identify them. These beliefs can be negative thoughts that you have about money, such as "Money is the root of all evil" or "I'll never be able to earn enough money." Take a moment to reflect on your thoughts and beliefs about money, write them down, and examine how they affect your financial decisions.

Challenge your beliefs: Once you have identified your limiting beliefs, challenge them. Ask yourself if they are true or if they are based on assumptions or past experiences. For example, if you believe that "Money is the root of all evil," challenge this belief by asking yourself if money itself is evil or if it's the way people use money that can be evil.

Replace negative beliefs with positive ones: Once you have challenged your limiting beliefs, replace them with positive beliefs. For example, instead of saying "I'll never be able to earn enough money," say "I am capable of earning more money by learning new skills and taking on more opportunities."

Surround yourself with positive influences: Surround yourself with people who have a positive attitude towards money and success. Read books and articles about successful people who have overcome financial obstacles and achieved financial freedom.

Take action: Finally, take action to overcome your limiting beliefs. Start by setting financial goals, creating a budget, and educating yourself about money management. Take small steps towards your goals and celebrate your achievements along the way.

Changing negative money habits

Changing negative money habits can be a challenging task, but it's essential for improving your financial well-being and achieving financial stability. Negative money habits can include overspending, living beyond your means, failing to save, and not keeping track of your finances. In this response, we will discuss some strategies for changing negative money habits.

Identify the negative money habit: The first step to changing any negative behavior is to identify the habit that needs changing. Take time to evaluate your spending habits and identify areas where you are overspending, failing to save, or not making wise financial decisions.

Set clear financial goals: Setting clear financial goals is an excellent way to motivate yourself to change negative money habits. Establishing specific and measurable financial goals can help you focus your efforts and stay on track.

Create a budget: Creating a budget is a fundamental step towards changing negative money habits. A budget will help you track your expenses, plan for your future, and identify areas where you can cut back on spending.

Track your spending: Keeping track of your spending is crucial for changing negative money habits. You need to know where your money is going, what you are spending it on, and how much you are spending to make informed financial decisions.

Reduce unnecessary expenses: One of the most effective ways to change negative money habits is to reduce unnecessary expenses. Look for areas where you can cut back on spending, such as dining out, buying coffee, or subscribing to services that you don't use.

Develop healthy financial habits:
Developing healthy financial habits can help you overcome negative money habits. Some healthy financial habits include setting up automatic savings, paying bills on time, and avoiding impulse purchases.

Seek professional help: If you are struggling to change your negative money habits, seek professional help. A financial advisor can help you develop a personalized plan to manage your finances and achieve your financial goals.

Practicing gratitude and abundance

Practicing gratitude and abundance are two powerful practices that can have a positive impact on our mental, emotional, and physical well-being. Gratitude is the practice of being thankful and appreciative of what we have in our lives, while abundance is the belief that there is more than enough of everything we need in life. In this response, we will discuss these two practices in more detail, their benefits, and how to incorporate them into our daily lives.

Gratitude is a practice that involves consciously recognizing and appreciating the good things in our lives, whether they are big or small. When we practice gratitude regularly, we can experience a range of benefits. Research has shown that gratitude can improve our relationships, increase our happiness and life satisfaction, reduce stress and anxiety, improve our physical health, and even help us sleep better.

There are many ways to practice gratitude. One simple way is to keep a gratitude journal, where you write down three things you are grateful for each day. This can help shift our focus away from what we lack and towards what we have, cultivating a sense of contentment and satisfaction in our lives. Another way is to express gratitude to others, whether it's through a thank-you note, a verbal expression of appreciation, or a small gift. Gratitude can also be practiced through meditation, where we focus our attention on the present moment and the things we are grateful for.

Abundance, on the other hand, is the belief that there is more than enough of everything we need in life, whether it's love, wealth, health, or any other resource. When we cultivate a mindset of abundance, we can feel more empowered, optimistic, and motivated to take action towards our goals. Abundance thinking is the opposite of scarcity thinking, which is the belief that there is never enough and that we are always lacking something.

To cultivate abundance, we can start by focusing on what we already have, rather than what we lack. We can practice affirmations that reinforce our belief in abundance, such as "there is always enough" or "I am worthy of abundance." We can also take action towards our goals and trust that the universe will provide us with the resources we need along the way.

Practicing gratitude and abundance together can be a powerful combination. When we focus on what we have and appreciate it, we can attract more abundance into our lives. Conversely, when we cultivate a mindset of abundance, we can feel more grateful for the blessings we already have. By practicing these two habits together, we can create a virtuous cycle of positivity and well-being in our lives.

Chapter 5: Increasing Your Income and Creating Multiple Streams of Income

Advancing in your career

Advancing in one's career is an important goal for many professionals. It can provide a sense of achievement, increased job satisfaction, and financial rewards. However, advancing in one's career can be a complex and challenging process. In this response, I will discuss some strategies and considerations for advancing in your career.

Set clear career goals: Before you can begin to advance in your career, you must have a clear understanding of what you want to achieve. It's important to set specific and measurable goals that align with your skills, interests, and values. For example, you may want to become a team leader, take on more responsibilities, or switch to a different industry.

Develop your skills: To advance in your career, you need to have the skills and knowledge that are in demand in your industry. This may involve getting additional training or education, attending conferences or workshops, or seeking out mentors who can help you develop your skills. Keep up-to-date with the latest trends and technologies in your field and identify opportunities to learn new skills.

Network: Building relationships with people in your industry is critical for advancing in your career. Attend industry events, join professional associations, and participate in online communities to connect with like-minded professionals. Be proactive in reaching out to people you admire and ask for their advice or mentorship.

Seek out opportunities: To advance in your career, you need to be willing to take on new challenges and responsibilities. Look for opportunities to lead projects, volunteer for assignments that stretch your skills, or take on temporary assignments that can give you exposure to different parts of the organization.

Communicate effectively: Effective communication is essential for advancing in your career. Be clear about your goals and expectations, and communicate your achievements and contributions to your colleagues and managers. Practice active listening, seek feedback, and be open to constructive criticism.

Stay positive and adaptable: Advancing in your career can be a long and sometimes challenging journey. Stay positive, focus on your strengths, and be open to feedback and opportunities for growth. Be adaptable and willing to pivot your career goals as needed based on changes in your industry or personal circumstances.

Starting a side business or freelancing

Starting a side business or freelancing is a great way to create additional income streams, gain new skills, and explore your passions. In recent years, there has been a significant increase in the number of people starting side businesses or working as freelancers. This is largely due to the rise of the gig economy and the availability of online platforms that make it easy to connect with clients and customers from all over the world.

Benefits of Starting a Side Business or Freelancing:

Additional Income: One of the most significant benefits of starting a side business or freelancing is the potential for additional income. This can help you pay off debt, save for retirement, or even achieve financial independence.

Flexibility: Another advantage of starting a side business or freelancing is the flexibility it provides. You can work on your business or projects during your free time, and you have the flexibility to set your own schedule. This is particularly appealing to those who have a full-time job or other commitments that make it difficult to work a traditional 9-5 schedule.

Pursue Your Passion: Starting a side business or freelancing also allows you to pursue your passions and interests. You can turn your hobbies or interests into a profitable venture, which can be incredibly rewarding.

Learn New Skills: When starting a side business or freelancing, you will inevitably learn new skills that can be useful in other areas of your life or career. For example, you may learn about marketing, financial management, or project management.

Challenges of Starting a Side Business or Freelancing:

Time Constraints: One of the biggest challenges of starting a side business or freelancing is finding the time to work on it. Balancing your full-time job, personal life, and your business can be challenging, and it requires careful planning and time management skills.

Financial Risk: Starting a side business or freelancing also comes with financial risks. There may be upfront costs associated with starting your business, and there is no guarantee that you will make a profit. It's important to have a solid business plan and financial projections to help mitigate these risks.

Self-Motivation: As a side business owner or freelancer, you are responsible for your own motivation and productivity. It can be challenging to stay motivated and focused, especially when you are working alone.

Tips for Starting a Side Business or Freelancing:

Identify Your Niche: Before starting a side business or freelancing, it's important to identify your niche and target market. This will help you focus your efforts and develop a clear value proposition.

Develop a Business Plan: Developing a business plan is essential when starting a side business or freelancing. This will help you define your goals, target market, and financial projections.

Set Realistic Goals: When starting a side business or freelancing, it's important to set realistic goals and expectations. Don't expect to make a full-time income right away, and be prepared to put in the time and effort required to build your business.

Build Your Online Presence: In today's digital age, having a strong online presence is essential for any business or freelancer. This includes building a website, creating social media profiles, and networking with potential clients or customers.

Seek Support: Starting a side business or freelancing can be challenging, so it's important to seek support from friends, family, or mentors. You may also want to consider joining a community of like-minded entrepreneurs or freelancers for additional support and guidance.

Investing in real estate or other passive income streams

Investing in real estate or other passive income streams can be an effective way to generate additional income and build wealth over the long term. Both options offer potential benefits and drawbacks, and it is important to carefully evaluate each investment opportunity before making a decision.

Investing in Real Estate

Real estate investment can be an attractive option for those looking to diversify their portfolio. Real estate investments can provide steady cash flow through rental income and can also appreciate in value over time, offering the potential for capital gains. There are various ways to invest in real estate, including direct ownership of rental properties, real estate investment trusts (REITs), and crowdfunding platforms.

Direct ownership of rental properties can offer the potential for high returns but also requires significant time and effort to manage and maintain the property. REITs provide a more passive investment option, allowing investors to purchase shares in a portfolio of properties and receive a share of the rental income generated. Crowdfunding platforms provide opportunities for investors to participate in real estate investments with lower minimum investment amounts, but also come with additional risk.

Other Passive Income Streams

There are various other passive income streams that investors can consider, including dividend stocks, bonds, peer-to-peer lending, and other alternative investments. Each option comes with its own set of risks and potential rewards.

Dividend stocks can offer a consistent stream of income through regular dividend payments. However, it is important to carefully evaluate the company's financial health and dividend history before investing.

Bonds can also provide a reliable source of income, with the added benefit of lower risk compared to stocks. However, the returns may be lower than other investments.

Peer-to-peer lending platforms offer opportunities for investors to lend money to individuals or small businesses and earn interest on their investment. However, this option comes with higher risk and may require additional research and due diligence.

Other alternative investments such as cryptocurrency, art, or collectibles can offer the potential for high returns, but also come with greater risk and volatility.

Factors to Consider

Before investing in real estate or other passive income streams, it is important to consider a few key factors:

Risk tolerance: Each investment comes with its own level of risk, and it is important to evaluate your risk tolerance before making any investment decisions.

Investment goals: Determine your investment goals and time horizon before investing. Are you looking for a short-term or long-term investment?

Diversification: Diversification is key to minimizing risk and maximizing returns. Consider diversifying your investments across different asset classes and industries.

Investment fees: It is important to carefully evaluate the fees associated with each investment opportunity to ensure they align with your investment goals and expected returns.

Building a personal brand and monetizing your skills

Building a personal brand and monetizing your skills is a popular trend in today's fast-paced world. Personal branding is the process of creating a unique identity and reputation for yourself, while monetizing your skills involves turning your talents into a profitable business or career. In this response, we will discuss the steps involved in building a personal brand and monetizing your skills.

Step 1: Define Your Brand

To build a strong personal brand, you need to have a clear understanding of who you are and what you stand for. This means defining your core values, mission statement, and unique selling proposition (USP). Your USP is what sets you apart from others in your field. It's the unique combination of skills, experiences, and personality traits that make you stand out.

Step 2: Identify Your Target Audience

Once you've defined your brand, it's important to identify your target audience. Who are you trying to reach? What are their needs and desires? Understanding your target audience is key to building a successful personal brand.

Step 3: Create Your Online Presence

In today's digital age, having a strong online presence is essential for building a personal brand. This includes creating a website, social media profiles, and a blog. Your website should showcase your skills and experiences, while your social media profiles should be used to engage with your audience and promote your brand.

Step 4: Network and Build Relationships

Networking and building relationships is crucial to building a successful personal brand. Attend industry events, join professional organizations, and connect with others in your field on social media. These relationships can lead to new opportunities and collaborations.

Step 5: Monetize Your Skills

Once you've built a strong personal brand, it's time to monetize your skills. This can involve starting a business, freelancing, or offering consulting services. You can also create and sell digital products such as e-books, online courses, or webinars.

To monetize your skills effectively, you need to be able to communicate the value you offer to potential clients. This means developing a pricing strategy, creating a portfolio of work, and being able to clearly articulate the benefits of working with you.

Chapter 6: Protecting Your Wealth and Planning for the Future

Estate planning basics

Estate planning is the process of creating a plan for managing and distributing your assets after your death. It involves making decisions about who will inherit your property, how your assets will be managed and distributed, and who will make decisions on your behalf if you become incapacitated. Here are some estate planning basics to consider:

Create a will: A will is a legal document that outlines how your assets will be distributed after your death. It can also name guardians for minor children and an executor to manage the estate. A will is a critical component of any estate plan.

Consider a trust: A trust is a legal entity that can hold assets for the benefit of a beneficiary. Trusts can be revocable or irrevocable and can help avoid probate, reduce taxes, and protect assets from creditors.

Designate beneficiaries: You can name beneficiaries for your retirement accounts, life insurance policies, and other assets. These beneficiaries will receive the assets after your death, regardless of what your will says.

Plan for incapacity: In addition to planning for your death, you should also plan for the possibility that you may become incapacitated. You can create a durable power of attorney and a health care directive to name someone to make financial and medical decisions on your behalf.

Consider tax implications: Estate planning can have significant tax implications. You should work with a tax professional to ensure that your estate plan is structured in a way that minimizes taxes.

Review and update your plan: Your estate plan should be reviewed and updated periodically, especially after major life events such as marriage, divorce, or the birth of a child.

Work with an estate planning professional: Estate planning can be complex, and it's important to work with an experienced professional to ensure that your plan is comprehensive and meets your goals.

Protecting your assets with insurance

Insurance is a form of risk management that provides financial protection against potential losses or damages. It is designed to protect individuals and businesses from the financial burden of unexpected events that may arise. Assets are a vital part of our lives and protecting them with insurance is essential. Here are some ways that insurance can protect your assets:

Property insurance: This type of insurance protects your physical assets such as your home, car, or other valuable belongings. It provides coverage in case of damage or loss due to natural disasters, theft, or accidents.

Liability insurance: This type of insurance provides coverage in case someone is injured on your property or if you are held liable for damages caused by your actions. It can also protect you from lawsuits, legal fees, and settlements.

Health insurance: This type of insurance provides financial protection in case of unexpected medical expenses. It can cover doctor visits, hospitalization, prescription medication, and other medical expenses.

Life insurance: This type of insurance provides financial support for your loved ones in case of your unexpected death. It can provide financial support for things like funeral expenses, outstanding debts, and living expenses for your family.

Disability insurance: This type of insurance provides financial protection in case of an injury or illness that leaves you unable to work. It can provide income replacement to help cover living expenses while you recover.

By having insurance, you can protect your assets from unexpected losses and ensure that you are financially secure in the event of an accident or disaster. It can provide peace of mind knowing that you and your family are protected in case of unexpected events. However, it is essential to carefully consider the coverage you need and choose a policy that meets your specific needs and budget.

To protect your assets with insurance, it is essential to do the following:

Evaluate your risks: Identify the potential risks that could affect your assets and consider the likelihood of them occurring. For example, if you live in an area prone to natural disasters, you may need to consider property insurance that covers those types of events.

Determine your coverage needs: Once you have identified your risks, determine the coverage you need to adequately protect your assets. Work with an insurance professional to help you determine the right coverage for your needs.

Shop around: Don't settle for the first insurance policy you come across. Shop around and compare different policies and premiums to find the best coverage for your needs and budget.

Review your coverage regularly: As your circumstances change, so too may your insurance needs. Review your coverage regularly to ensure that you are adequately protected and make adjustments as needed.

Retirement planning and saving for the future

Retirement planning and saving for the future is a critical aspect of financial planning. Retirement planning is the process of identifying your financial goals for retirement and developing a strategy to achieve those goals. Saving for the future is the act of setting aside money for a specific purpose, such as retirement, education, or a down payment on a house. We will discuss the importance of retirement planning and saving for the future, as well as the strategies that can be used to achieve these goals.

Importance of Retirement Planning and Saving for the Future:

Retirement planning and saving for the future is important for several reasons:

Financial Security: Retirement planning helps to ensure that you have enough money to support your lifestyle during your retirement years. This can help to provide financial security and peace of mind.

Compound Interest: By starting to save early and investing your money wisely, you can take advantage of compound interest. This means that your money will earn interest on the interest that has already been earned, which can lead to significant growth over time.

Inflation: Inflation is the rate at which the cost of goods and services increases over time. Saving for the future can help you to keep pace with inflation and ensure that your money retains its value over time.

Retirement Lifestyle: Retirement planning can help you to achieve your desired retirement lifestyle. This may include travel, hobbies, and other activities that require a significant amount of money.

Strategies for Retirement Planning and Saving for the Future:

Start Early: The earlier you start saving for retirement, the more time your money has to grow. Even small contributions can add up over time, thanks to the power of compound interest.

Set Goals: Determine how much money you will need to achieve your desired retirement lifestyle and set goals to help you achieve those targets.

Save Regularly: Consistently setting aside a portion of your income for retirement can help you build a sizeable nest egg over time.

Invest Wisely: Consider investing in a diversified portfolio of stocks, bonds, and other assets that are appropriate for your age, risk tolerance, and retirement goals.

Maximize Retirement Accounts: Take advantage of tax-advantaged retirement accounts, such as 401(k)s, IRAs, and Roth IRAs, to help you maximize your retirement savings.

Manage Debt: Avoid taking on excessive debt, which can hamper your ability to save for retirement and achieve your financial goals.

Seek Professional Advice: Consider working with a financial planner or advisor who can help you develop a retirement plan that is tailored to your specific needs and goals.

Legacy planning and charitable giving

Legacy planning and charitable giving are two important aspects of estate planning that involve the transfer of wealth or assets to future generations or charitable organizations. Legacy planning is the process of creating a plan that outlines how an individual's assets will be distributed after their death, while charitable giving is the act of donating money or assets to charitable organizations.

Legacy planning involves several key considerations, including the type of assets being transferred, the tax implications of the transfer, and the goals and objectives of the individual. Some common strategies used in legacy planning include wills, trusts, and gifts. A will is a legal document that outlines how an individual's assets will be distributed after their death, while a trust is a legal entity that can hold and manage assets on behalf of the beneficiaries. Gifts, on the other hand, are transfers of assets during an individual's lifetime.

Charitable giving is another important aspect of estate planning that involves the donation of money or assets to charitable organizations. Charitable giving can be done during an individual's lifetime or after their death through their will or trust. Charitable giving can provide a number of benefits, including tax advantages and the opportunity to support causes that are important to the individual.

There are several ways to engage in charitable giving, including direct donations, donor-advised funds, and charitable trusts. Direct donations involve giving money or assets directly to a charitable organization. Donor-advised funds are accounts that allow individuals to make contributions to a charitable organization and receive a tax deduction, while also retaining some control over how the funds are distributed. Charitable trusts, such as charitable remainder trusts and charitable lead trusts, are legal entities that can be used to provide income to the individual or their beneficiaries while also benefiting a charitable organization.

One important consideration for both legacy planning and charitable giving is the tax implications of the transfer. Depending on the type of assets being transferred and the value of those assets, there may be tax consequences that need to be taken into account. It is important to work with a qualified financial advisor or estate planning attorney to ensure that the transfer is structured in a way that maximizes the benefits to the individual and their beneficiaries.

Conclusion

Embracing your wealth is a critical step in achieving a more fulfilling life. While wealth alone may not guarantee happiness, it can provide individuals with greater opportunities and resources to pursue their passions, create meaningful experiences, and make a positive impact on the world around them.

However, embracing wealth does not mean being consumed by it. Instead, individuals must develop a healthy relationship with money, one that recognizes its importance without allowing it to define their sense of self-worth or happiness. They must also prioritize their values and use their wealth in ways that align with their beliefs, whether that means supporting a charitable cause, investing in their education, or traveling to new places.

Moreover, embracing wealth means taking responsibility for its impact on others and the world. It involves recognizing that with wealth comes privilege and power, and using those resources to make a positive impact on the lives of others. This might include supporting social justice initiatives, promoting sustainable practices, or advocating for positive change in the world.

Ultimately, embracing wealth is not about accumulating as much money as possible, but rather about using it to create a fulfilling and meaningful life. By cultivating a healthy relationship with money, prioritizing one's values, and using wealth to make a positive impact on the world, individuals can embrace their wealth and live a more fulfilling life.

www.ingramcontent.com/pod-product-compliance
Lightning Source LLC
Chambersburg PA
CBHW070439220526
45466CB00004B/1737